The Golden Chain of Homer

By

Anton Josef Kirchweger

Copyright © 2021 Lamp of Trismegistus. All rights reserved. No part of this publication may be reproduced or transmitted in any form or by any means, electronic or mechanical, including photocopying, recording, or by any information storage and retrieval system, without permission in writing from Lamp of Trismegistus. Reviewers may quote brief passages.

ISBN: 978-1-63118-524-3

Esoteric Classics:
Studies in Alchemy

Other Books in this Series and Related Titles

Aurora of the Philosophers by Paracelsus (978-1-63118-507-6)

The Secret Book of the Philosopher's Stone by Artephius (978-1-63118-517-5)

Rosicrucian Rules, Secret Signs, Codes and Symbols by various (978-1-63118-488-8)

On the Philadelphian Gold by Philochrysus & Philadelphus (978-1-63118-511-3)

Paracelsus, the Four Elements and Their Spirits by M P Hall (978-1-63118-400-0)

Book of Vexations by Paracelsus (978-1-63118-520-5)

Hermetic Arcanum by Jean d'Espagnet (978-1-63118-519-9)

The Stone of the Philosophers by A E Waite (978-1-63118-509-0)

The Magician's Heavenly Chaos by Thomas Vaughan (978-1-63118-500-7)

Freher's Process in the Philosophical Work by D A Freher (978-1-63118-484-0)

The Rosicrucian Chemical Marriage by Christian Rosenkreuz (978-1-63118-458-1)

The Alchemical Catechism of Paracelsus by Paracelsus (978-1-63118-513-7)

Alchemy in the Nineteenth Century by Helena P. Blavatsky (978-1-63118-446-8)

Rosicrucians and Speculative Masonry in the Seventeenth Century (978-1-63118-489-5)

The Sepher Yetzirah and the Qabalah by M P Hall (978-1-63118-481-9)

The Devil in Love by Jacques Cazotte (978–1–63118–499–4)

Crystal Vision Through Crystal Gazing by Frater Achad (978-1-63118-455-0)

The Golden Verses of Pythagoras: Five Translations (978-1-63118-479-6)

Arcane Formulas or Mental Alchemy by W W Atkinson (978-1-63118-459-8)

The A E Waite Reader: A Selection of Occult Essays (978-1-63118-515-1)

The Leadbeater Reader: A Selection of Occult Essays (978-1-63118-483-3)

Audio versions are also available on Audible, Amazon and Apple

Other Books in this Series and Related Titles

On the Cave of the Nymphs in the Odyssey by Thomas Taylor (978-1-63118-505-2)

The Poem of Hashish by A Crowley & C Baudelaire (978-1-63118-484-0)

With the Adepts or An Adventure Among the Rosicrucians (978-1-63118-523-6)

The Kabbalah of Masonry & Related Writings by E Levi &c (978-1-63118-453-6)

A Collection of Fiction and Essays by Occult Writers on Supernatural and Metaphysical Subjects by various (978–1–63118–510–6)

Clairvoyance and Psychic Abilities by A Besant &c (978-1-63118-403-1)

Cloud Upon the Sanctuary by Waite & K Eckartshausen (978-1-63118-438-3)

The Hymns of Hermes by G. R. S. Mead (978-1-63118-405-5)

The Secrets of Enoch by Enoch (978-1-63118-449-9)

Masonic and Rosicrucian History by M P Hall & H Voorhis (978-1-63118-486-4)

The Sword of Welleran and Other Stories by Lord Dunsany (978-1-63118-501-4)

The Janeites, The Man Who Would Be King and Other Stories of Freemasonry by Rudyard Kipling (978–1–63118–480–2)

A Weird Tale & Other Supernatural Stories by W Q Judge (978-1-63118-518-2)

The First and Second Gospels of the Infancy of Jesus Christ (978-1-63118-415-4)

The Life of Pythagoras by Porphyry (978-1-63118-512-0)

Freemasonry & Catholicism by Max Heindel (978-1-63118-508-3)

The Feminine Occult by various authors (978-1-63118-711-7)

Qabbalistic Teachings and the Tree of Life by M P Hall (978-1-63118-482-6)

The Influence of Pythagoras on Freemasonry and Other Essays (978-1-63118-404-8)

The Path of Light: A Manual of Maha-Yana Buddhism (978-1-63118-471-0)

Tao Te Ching & Commentary by Lao Tzu & C Johnston (978-1-63118-495-6)

Audio versions are also available on Audible, Amazon and Apple

Table of Contents

Introduction…7

1 *What Nature is*…9
2 *How All Things Proceed Therefrom*…10
3 *How All Things are Further Generated*…14
4 *How the Universal Sperm is Generated by the Four Elements*…16
5 *In What Manner the Divided Chaotic Water is Regenerated and Becomes the Universal and General Sperm of All Things, Called Anima or Spiritus Mundi*…19
6 *Of the Heavens and Their Influence*…21
7 *Of the Atmosphere or Air and its Influence*…24
8 *Of Water and its Effluvium*…26
9 *Of the Earth and its Effluvium*…28
10 *Discovery of the Genuine Universal Sperm in the Regenerated Chaos, the Corporified Animal or Spiritus Mundi*…33
11 *The Nitre and Salt are Found in the Air and in All Things in This World*…43
12 *That There is Nitre and Salt in All Waters and Earths*…48
13 *That nitre and salt is found in Animals, that Animals proceed from nitre and salt, and are resolved into nitre and salt*…51
14 *That nitre and salt is found in Vegetables; that Vegetables consist of nitre and salt, and are resolved into nitre and salt*…52
15 *That nitre and salt is found in Minerals; that Minerals are formed of nitre and salt, and are resolved into nitre and salt*…54
16 *Of the principal Gate Key to Nature, the author of destruction and regeneration of all things, called Putrefaction*…59
17 *What Putrefaction is*…61

INTRODUCTION

The word "esoteric" can be difficult to define. Esotericism in general can be seen less as a system of beliefs and more as a category, which encompasses numerous, different systems of beliefs. It's a bit of juxtaposition, since the word "esoteric" indicates something that few people know about, while the term itself broadly covers numerous philosophies, practices, areas of study and belief systems.

In a greater sense, Esotericism acts as a storehouse for secret knowledge, which is often considered ancient (*by tradition, if not by fact*), passed down from generation to generation, in private. At various times in history, simply possessing the knowledge of some of these subjects, was considered illegal and a jailable offence, if discovered. This usually included such general topics as Alchemy, Pharmacology, Qabalah, Hermeticism, Occultism, Ceremonial Magic, Astrology, Divination, Rosicrucianism and so on. Collectively, these areas of study were often referred to as the esoteric sciences.

Sometimes, the outer garment of a subject isn't esoteric, while what is hidden beneath it, is. As an example, Freemasonry isn't necessarily esoteric by nature (at *least not anymore*), but certain signs, passwords and handshakes given to the candidate during their initiation, are in fact, esoteric, in the sense that they are hidden from the general public.

Today, in the twenty-first century, such topics are readily available at bookstores across the country, and numerous mainsteam publishers offer beginners guides and coffee-table volumes on many of these subjects, intended for mass appeal. Books like *"The Secret"* have turned previously arcane topics into household knowledge. All that being the case, however, it isn't to say that there still aren't buried secrets to uncover, ancient wisdom being ignored and forgotten mysteries to be explored. In fact, it is often that we are only able to further our own studies by standing on the shoulders of these disappearing giants.

Lamp of Trismegistus is doing its part to help preserve humanity's esoteric history by making some of these classics available to those students who are seeking to unearth the knowledge of these ancient colossi.

So, be sure to check other titles from our *Esoteric Classics* series, as well as our *Occult Fiction*, *Theosophical Classics*, *Foundations of Freemasonry Series*, *Supernatural Fiction*, *Paranormal Research Series*, *Studies in Buddhism* and our *Christian Apocrypha Series*. You can also download the audio versions of most of these titles from Amazon, Apple or Audible, for learning on the go.

AUREA CATENA HOMERI
THE GOLDEN CHAIN OF HOMER
OF THE GENERATION OF THINGS

Chapter 1

What Nature Is

Nature comprehends the visible and invisible Creatures of the Whole universe. What we call Nature especially, is the universal fire or Anima Mundi, filling the whole system of the Universe, and therefore is a Universal Agent, omnipresent, and endowed with an unerring instinct, and manifests itself in fire and Light. It is the First creature of Divine Omnipotence.

Chapter 2

How All Things Proceed Therefrom

Thus God created first this invisible fire and endowed it with an unerring Instinct and a Capacity to manifest itself in 3 Principles.

1. In its Original most Universal state it is perfectly invisible, immaterial, cold and occupies no space, in this tranquil state it is of no use to us, yet in this unmoved state it is omnipresent.

2. In its second state it is manifested by motion or agitation into light. In this state it was separated out of the Chaos, when God said, "Let there be Light." Yet it is still cold. When gently moved or agitated, it manifests warmth and Heat, as in the case in all Frictions and in Fermentation of moist things.

3. When collected in a sufficient quantity, and violently agitated it is manifested into burning fire. This continues burning as long as it is agitated, and has a fit subject to act upon; when that fails, it returns to its first state of tranquil Universality. In the character of burning fire it manifests Light and Heat. Thus,

(a) we say in its first most Universal state it is perfectly invisible and immaterial.

(b) In its second state of manifestation it is visible in Light, but remains cold and immaterial.

(c) In its third state of Heat and burning fire it is visible, hot or burning, and becomes somewhat material as it occupies Room or Space whilst in this State.

You have seen how 3 distinct powers of the Universal Spirit, but it possesses still more and even some inconceivable powers.

We have told you that the Universal spirit endowed with an unerring Instinct, working by the most simple and nearest way, it has, also, besides its already mentioned conspicuous qualities, two occult powers, viz: attracting and repulsing, and these two powers are inconceivably great!

We see various instances of it in Thunder and Lightning, in Earthquakes, Hurricanes and in the surprising effects of Gunpowder.

When God created this Universal fire, He gave it a power to become material, that is to become Vapour, Humidity, water and earth, although that fire in its own Universal Nature, is, and remains centrally the same. Thus you see the Beginning of the 4 Elements, viz

(1) burning fire; Vapour or Humidity mixed with Cold fire constitutes atmospheric air,

(2) air, which still more condensed becomes water,

(3) and water inspissated becomes earth.

Originally it was but one Element Fire.

Thus the Universal fire became a Vapour of immense Extent, which by further inspissation became chaotic water, and out of this Chaotic Water the Creator separated the Light, that is: separated the Universal invisible fire into Light. Thus we see here that Universal, at first invisible fire manifested in two Principles, Light and Humidity!

Therefore out of Light and water, God has created all Things.

Water was the first condensation or corporification of the Universal fire, which water nevertheless in its center was, and remains fire, full of life and activity, and the more so, as it was assisted by its Equal, the Light, separated out of it, as much as was necessary for the creating of all immaterial and material Beings, and in success of time for their maintenance.

Of the separated Light we have spoken before, we have now to consider its first body Humidity or water. This water differs it regard to Rarefaction or Density; if Rarefied to a certain Degree it constitutes air, that is fire predominating above water, but if condensed to a degree it becomes Humid water, or Humidity predominating above fire. Nevertheless, in both, that is in their Center lays concealed fire or the Universal spirit.

As soon as the air gets deprived of its Universal fire, which animates it and renders it elastic, it becomes immediately putrid, and thereby declines lower down, becomes Humidity, mud, earth and immoveable; it is the same case with water when deprived of fire, or of animated air, it becomes putride, condenses still further and becomes earth, immoveable.

God has ordained it so that the Universal spirit by means of Humidity should work all things, because Humidity mixes easily with everything, by means of which the spirit can soften, penetrate, generate. destroy and regenerate all things.

Thus Humidity or water is the Body, the Vehicle and Tool, but the spirit or fire is the Operator, the Universal Agent and fabricator of all Natural Things.

This universal fire fills that immense space in the Universe between the heavenly bodies. and as it has a power to become material, it generates a subtil vapour or invisible most subtil Humidity, its first passive principle: It causes therein a gentle Reaction, and a general, gentle, most subtil Fermentation takes place Universally, and by this Reaction the Universal Acid is everywhere generated, which we can deem nothing else than a most subtil incorporeal Nitre Spiritus Mundi, outwardly cold and inwardly fire. Thus this Spiritual incorporeal Nitre or Universal Acid; we deem the second invisible change of the Universal fire, generated out of chaotic invisible Humidity: and as this approaches the atmospheres of the heavenly bodies, it becomes gradually more and more material, until it meets an alcaline passive principle wherein it fixes itself and forms Native nitre, so that from Spiritus Mundi, it becomes nitre.

Thus we say, not without good reason, that the Solar Rays of Light, are nothing else but a most subtil spiritual Spiritual Mundi, which gradually becomes more and more nitreous, as it approaches the Earth, but Sea Salt in the Ocean; animating the atmosphere with fire or Life, and thereby giving elasticity to the air, and Life and preservation to the water. From this, every man of common understanding may learn what Nature is, and its origin.

We see that between the Firmament and our Earth continual Vapours, Clouds, and Fogs, which ascend like a transpiration of the Earth, and are sublimed upwards by the Central heat of the Earth. This Chaotic water and Vapours, contain, and are the First Matter of all Things, and although this appears very simple before our Eyes, yet it is two-fold, as it contains fire and Humidity, the Invisible in the Visible, the fire or spirit is the Agent, and the water the Patient.

Whosoever wishes to arrive at the Fountain of Secret Wisdom, let him mind this well; and let him go with this Central Point of Truth to the circumference, and for ever imprint in his memory: that from fire and water, or spirit enclosed in Humidity all things in the World are generated, preserved, destroyed and regenerated.

Whosoever comprehends this well will find no difficulty in analising Natural things as he may easily volatilize fixt, and fix the volatile: a stinking subject he may convert into a pleasant smelling one, out of poison he can make a salutary Medicine because he knows that all things proceed from one Root; and return to that Root: The distinction is external and regards only the modification of the Matter, which is more or less digested or fixt. Therefore the Philosophers say that their Matter is in all Things, yet they have selected such Subjects wherein the Universal spirit is more abundantly contained and more concentrated, and easer to be obtained; otherwise that spirit is All in All.

Chapter 3

How All Things Are Further Generated

We have demonstrated that the primordial Vapour, or that fire and water, are after God, the First Matter of all Things. This two-fold Vapour by inspissation is become water and this water by the action of the invisible spirit therein diffused, has begun to ferment and then to generate Matter. At first, this water was perfectly subtil and pure, but by means of the action of the inward spirit, it becomes turbid, smelled badly and thus generated Earth. It was divided into various parts. into a Spiritual, most subtil, into a half or less subtil, into a half corporeal, and into a Body. At first it was 1 and 2, -- now it is 1, 2, and 3, likewise 4 and 5.

It was 1, as a simple Humidity;

2, as a water containing a spirit;

3, when it was separated into volatile, half fixt, and fixt, that is, chemically speaking -- into Volatil, Acetum and Alcali; Anima, spirit, Corpus;

4, when it was divided into the four so-called Elements, fire, air, water, earth;

5, when it is by Art, assisted by Nature, formed into an indestructible fiery Quintessence, thus [unidentified symbol].

When the water has attained to its term of putrefaction, we may separate one subtil after another; the most subtil will certainly ascend before the less subtil, and so one principle after another until the least volatile comes last.

God had ordained that the different modifications of the Universal spirit, in the four Elements, should continually generate and produce a Universal General Sperm, for that reason God has given to each individual thing its Agent and Patient, in order to cause a Reaction; This we see by the evaporation of numberless Subjects, who send forth whatever Humidity then have more than is necessary. This evaporation when from above is called Influence, but when from things here below it is called Effluvium.

God has given each Individual its particular Sperm. which however all depends on the Universal Sperm, as their Ruler and Conductor.

Chapter 4

How the Universal Sperm Is Generated by the Four Elements

After God had divided or corporified the Anima or Spirit Mundi, the simple Chaos into four Elements. or predominating, leading principles; He called to them "increase and multiply"; The Heavens and the Air, both animated by the Universal fire are the Father, the Male, the Agent or Operating principles. Water and earth are the Mother, the Female or Passive principle. These four are nevertheless only two, fire and water; They are forced to engender continually a regenerated Chaotic water or primordial Chaos out of their Center, for the generation, preservation, destruction and regeneration of all Things, and this will continue until it pleases God to Calcine and regenerate the whole Earth!

These four so-called Elements, which must fabricate the Universal Sperm or regenerate the Chaos, when one Extream is considered towards the other, seem quite contrary, and indeed as contraries they cannot effect any good; yet when they meet orderly, they are fully capable to execute that what God has ordained them for.

It is a natural and philosophical Axiom "Non transire posse abuno Extremo ad alterum absque medio," -- that is: It is impossible to proceed from one Extream to another Extream without a Medium. This Axiom every Artist ought to mind, thousands err because they do not observe this Truth.

Fire cannot become water without air, and earth cannot become air without water . If you would unite fire, as being extreamly volatile and subtil, with the earth, which is corporeal and fixt, you will never be able to do it; because the most Volatile will forsake the fixt and return to its Chaos. This is so in all Natural Things, that the most

Volatile principle, cannot unite with the most fixt without its proper medium. An Artist ought to observe this constantly that he may not lose his time, his Matter, and Expenses.

Therefore if you want to unite Heaven or fire with the earth, or convert fire into earth, unite it first with its nearest volatile medium and they will unite immediately, when that is done, give them the water, as a medium between air and earth, and they will also unite; then add the earth, and thus you may unite fire with earth and fix it therein; and so vice versa turn the earth into water with water, then convert it into air, and the air into fire by means of air.

The Heaven or fire is extreamly subtil, the air is also subtil, but one degree more corporeal than the fire; water is again a degree more corporeal than the air, and the earth is a degree more corporeal than the water. Thus we must proceed as Nature does, and we may then obtain a Quintessentificated Operation, if we do not mind this, we can do little or nothing.

Nature has its different degrees of subtilty, and mixes the most subtil fire with the less subtil, and that with the least subtil.

When they are united, they influence into the most subtil water, then into the less subtil, and into the grossest. Then it mixes gradually with the most subtil earth, with the less and least subtil, until it becomes Rocks and Stones.

In a chemical Anatomy we see how the most subtil comes over first, and how Nature regulates her Operations, and does not confound one principle with another, but lets go the most Volatile and most subtil first, and then the next less Volatile, and so on etc. for Example:

Take an earth out of a Field or Meadow or what Earth you please, pour Water upon it so as to dilate your Earth well, then let it stand a few days and you will find that the coarse heavy earth settles at the bottom of the Vessel, you must stir it 3 or 4 times a day. The water will in the meantime dissolve the most subtil earth which is its salt, this does unite with the water, as being a Virgin earth.

As soon as this salt, or Virgin earth is extracted out of the common earth, the water cannot dissolve it any further.

Now you must distil this water containing the salt, into a spiritual water, and you must cohobate so often until all the salt has come over with the water.

This water now has the power to dissolve again the next subtil earth, which can like the first salt be distilled over as a spiritual water.

With this Water you may proceed in dissolving more of the remaining earth, until by distillations and cohobations, you have dissolved the whole quantity and volatilised it into a spiritual water; This is a tedious Operation but of great moment: In the same manner Nature operates by dissolving and coagulating, until the Universal Sperm of all Things is generated, which is universal seed.

The Artist must observe that Nature proceeds gradually and regularly. and observes time weight, and measure, he must transpose the External into the Internal and Heavenly, and he will obtain more and more knowledge.

Chapter 5

In What Manner the Divided Chaotic Water Is Regenerated and Becomes the Universal and General Sperm of All Things, Called Anima or Spiritus Mundi

The 4 so-called Elements have been separated out of the Chaos, but they proceed all from one. The form is but one, and the Matter is but one. The form is fire, and the Matter is water.

The difference consists in their external appearance, by Fermentation fire becomes air, and air becomes water, and water is become earth; But when fire is fixed by Art or by Nature it becomes earth, and when the earth is volatilised by water it becomes air and fire.

Because one Element can be converted into the other, if this was not true they would differ centrally, but they do not. The Chaos which produced these Elements was in the beginning fire and water only, these two have been divided into four b a further volatilisation and Inspissation: By volatilisatian extennation or rerefaction, Humidity becomes air animated by fire, but by condensation in Inspissation of that Primordial Humidity the Earth has been formed with the fire turned downwards, toward the Center of the Earth. The Hieroglyphic characters of the Elements explain their nature exactly.

There is not a Subject under the Heavens, whether liquid or dry which does not contain this Universal fire, and Primordial Humidity. The first is called Innate Heat, -- the last is called Radical Humidity.

The Universal fire becomes Humidity externally, but remained fire internally; being internally extreamly spiritual and volatile, it was of course extreamly active and moveable, and by that primitive mobility, excited warmth and fermentation and by that fermentation the Universal vinegar was, and is continually generated, and when this meets with a proper Body, whether in water or in the earth the Universal Sperm becomes visible and Corporeal, but whilst it is only a Vapour in the atmosphere, it is then the Universal Astral and incorporeal Sperm. This is the influence we receive from Heaven by means of the Air.

The Heavens give their influence, so does the Air, Water and Earth, and with united efforts they fabricate continually the Universal Sperm of the World.

Chapter 6

Of the Heavens and Their Influence

Heaven, after the separation of the Chaos, is the first principle, and became visible in Light: It is the most subtil and the highest, as well as the most universal, when it generated Humidity it became a most subtil Vapour, pure and extreamly Volatile, for that reason occupies the highest Station, or the remotest from the atmospheres of the heavenly Bodies.

This most subtil principle is full of Life and the most active for which reason we call Heaven the first Agent, the Male Sperm the Soul, a subtle air, a subtil water, a volatile earth.

Heaven and air have their influence not upwards, but downwards, towards water and earth, but earth and water ascends upwards to meet them. They mix thus in the state of vapours in order to fabricate the Chaotic regenerated, and impregnated water or the Universal, Semi-material Sperma Mundi. As soon as the air is impregnated and animated with Heaven, it communicates immediately with water and earth to impregnate them also.

This communication is done in a moment, as the Elements are gradually prepared to meet and mix with each other, by a continual circulation. There is no doubt but our atmosphere is continually loaded with Vapours, exhalations and clouds for the sake of communication of the Elements; as soon as these Vapours become condensed into Rain, Dew, Snow or Hail and fall down that same moment the volatilisations and exhalations of water and earth take place and are ready to succeed and meet those, which come down; so that there can never be no want of generation of such Vapours, which when sufficiently dilated or extended constitute our common air, which is more or less pure according as it is more or less animated by Heaven or fire.

The Heavens receive the ascending Vapours, which as they recede from the atmosphere become more and more subtil and spiritual until they are actually returned to their first Universal state of Ether or Spiritus Mundi. The atmospheric air also receives continually the volatilised water and succeeding Vapours, until it is satiated and overloaded, when the superflous Humidity is forced down again in Dew, Rain, Hail, Snow.

Thus fire and air come down into the Waters and impregnate them; the Waters dispose their thickest part and give it to the Earth; the Earth thereby becomes overloaded or saturated, which superfluity of earth and water is again volatised and sublimed upwards by the fire, inverted fire or Central Heat, into Vapours, which ascension and descension God has implanted into the Universal fire, as the Great and only Agent of nature, or rather Nature herself which causes this perpetual circulation by its attracting and repulsing power, as we have demonstrated in the Second Chapter.

The Lover of Natural Knowledge may clearly learn here how the Effluvium of one Element becomes the food and nourishment of the others, until converted therein; the same takes place with us and our food, as, for instance, we eat Bread and drink Wine, we discharge the superfluities of our food, which are used for manure on the land; seed is sown therein and out of such superfluities grows again our food.

A Tree looses its leaves during Winter, the leaves fall to the Root, where they putrify and become humidity which penetrates to the Root and feeds the Tree again.

Observe this well and you will fully comprehend the Superius and Inferious of Hermes, and our Catena Homeri or Platonic Ring. Thus you will see a continual transmutation of Matter, that is a conditional change or modification, whilst the inward central fire of Nature remains always the same, as it was in the beginning. All things were water at first, and return to water . Apply this throughout our Book, which is no small step towards out Art.

Chapter 7

Of the Atmosphere or Air, and Its Influence

Air is the second principle after the separation of the Chaos, and is the Vehicle or Instrument of the first i.e. fire; We mean here the genuine animated air. This we call Male, Manly, Sperm, and first Operator in all Things.

The Heavens or fire is the Anima and Life whilst the air or extenuated, rarefied Humidity is the spirit and Receptacle of the Soul and Principle of Life, and consequently animated fire ought to be named Spiritus Vitalis Macrocosmi, or the Vital Spirit of the Earth which we inhabit.

Air is a most subtil humid vapour or rarefied water wherein fire dwells abundantly. This is more corporeal than the Ether beyond the Atmosphere, which Ether is totally unfit for Inspiration, as being too subtil to fill the air vesicles in the lungs of animals: Air being the genuine Medium between fire and water, as it partakes of both, is therefore capable to receive the most subtil celestial fiery influences as well as the sublimed vapours from below, and by a continual motion or circulation, more and more vapours are converted into air, and more and more of such air becomes animated by fire, and as soon as it is saturated, the superflous humidity is condensed again and comes down in the character of animated water, such is Rain, Dew, Hail, and Snow.

By this you see that atmospheric air is the first Medium to unite fire with water and earth, and without it the Heavens could never communicate with water and earth.

Thus air becomes vapour and water, and the thicker the water gets, the better it mixes with the Earth, as on the contrary the Earth by Subtilisation by means of water is again converted into air, Nature operating these perpetual changes and conversions from one extream to the other: When they unite in Vapours they fabricate the

Universal Sperm of the World Spiritus Mundi, which is partly resolved in Dew and Rain etc. and partly remains in the air for the sake of animation; the atmospheric animated Waters fall down upon the Earth, as the Receptacle of all Celestial virtues, and fertilises it, for the growth and nourishment of Animals, Vegetables and Minerals. The Earth itself is a condensed or fixed Heaven, and Heaven is a volatilised earth, air is a rarefied water, and water is condensed air. We have here to note that one Element differs from the other only in this, that the One is volatile, the Other fixed, the one is fluid or dissolved, the Other is condensed or coagulated, and yet every one is and remains centrally and inwardly what they all were at first, -- i.e. prima materia or fire; Lastly, the Air may be called Renes, or the Kidneys of the Macrocosm, because in the air is chiefly found the conflux of all radical substantial. macrocosmical fluids, and the pure Extract of Essence of the World does meet there, where that ancient primordial Chaos is daily and hourly generated and regenerated for generation, preservation, destruction and regeneration of all Natural Things.

What are Dew, Rain, Snow, or Hail else but a regenerated Chaos? Out of which Animals, Vegetables, and Minerals receive part of the vivifying principle and nourishment: and all this is generated in the Air.

Chaper 8

Of Water and Its Effluvium

Water and earth belong together, as fire and air do, nay, all four stand in need of each other; the earth wants water, and fire cannot do without air; air without or deprived of fire becomes a putrid humidity, and water without animated air becomes mud and earth.

Water is the third principle, but the first passive Element, the Female Sperm and Menstrum of the Macrocosm, which does the Office of conveying food and nourishment to all Sublunary Creatures, and is, with the Earth, the Mother of all Things. Water is condensed air and a fluid earth. Water is a Medium between air and earth.

As soon as fire is become air, and air been converted into water, Dew, Rain, or Snow, they fall down on the inferior grosser waters and earth and mix therewith, begin to ferment by means of the primogenial implanted spirit or fire, and one Element operates into the other, until they have produced their Fruit from convenient Matrixes.

Here the Artist may learn Wisdom from Nature, which is not satisfied with one Medium of Union, viz: air to convert fire into earth, but makes use of water also. Thus the Artist must follow Nature, if he wants to unite and fix his principles together; Let him look for a Medium of Union, which is easily found; and if one Medium is not enough, let him employ two, and if two prove inadequate, let him take three, but homogenials and not heterogenials, as minerals agree with minerals, vegetables with vegetables etc. Minerals agree also with Vegetables, and Vegetables with Animals, as the Vegetables stand between Animals and Minerals.

The difference between them all is but external, not central, as they proceed originally all from one and the same Universal spirit;

Minerals are fixt Vegetables, Vegetables are Volatile Minerals, and one kingdom is transmutable into the other, in regard to its internal qualities.

Men and Beasts make use of Vegetables for food, and by their inward nature, they change those Vegetables into flesh and Blood; now when man and beasts die, they are buried underground, and Vegetables are again produced, which receive by means of their fibres and roots mineral Vapours, which are thus converted again into Vegetables.

This is the true Pythagorean Metempsychosis. Vegetables again. when they putrefy, assume a nitreous saline nature which is dissolved by rain and carried downwards through the pores, into the earth, or into the Sea. if near hand, from whence it ascends again as a mineral vapour, and thus Vegetables are frequently changed into Minerals, as well as into Animals, although more frequently into animals. Heaven and Air are Male Sperm, water is the Female Sperm and Menstrum, the Earth is the Womb or Matrix, wherein the two first, by means of the third operate every Generation.

Chapter 9

Of the Earth and Its Effluvium

Earth is the fourth and last principle of the Chaos. It is the second passive Element, the Matrix, and Mother of all sublinary Creatures; earth is a coagulated fixt Heaven a coagulated fixt water, and condensed air. The Center and Receptacle of all the heavenly Influences and of the Universal Sperm, which takes here a Body as well as in the Ocean.

Heaven by its extream subtility, is of all Elements the most moveable and omnipresent; its own motion, on account of its subtility is imperceptible, although visible in Light; This Universal fire is never idle, but perpetually active, pervading all things, although its action is generally imperceptible. This is the original cause of all Motion in Nature it moves the most subtil Air on the outward superficies of the atmospheres of the opaque celestial Bodies. This outward subtil air set in Motion, moves the next towards the region of Clouds and Vapours, yet as the atmospheres grow gradually thicker, i.e. more loaded with Vapours, the nearer to Sea and Land, the Motion is successively and gradually slower.

That the air is moved by the Ether or fire, is observable on account of the constant motion of the atmosphere; that Air set in Motion moves the Waters is well known to those who navigate the Seas and Rivers. That Water moves the Earth appears by the Sand, Mud and Stones which the Waters move continually from one place to the other. Here the Water carries off, and in other places accumulates Sand and whole Shores: now every Motion manifests warmth of the omnipresent cold, Universal fire, where it be perceptible or imperceptible as this depends on circumstances; In living Animals this warmth occasioned by moving the omnipresent fire is perceptible enough, whilst that same Motion is imperceptible in Vegetables and in Minerals. All Life proceeds from a Motion of the Universal fire, as a total privation of action and warmth extinguishes Life. From this let the Student collect that there exists a perceptible and imperceptible warmth.

This we tell you because in all the Elements exist Innate Heat, which is sometimes observable at other times not, this is not always dependent on the collected Rays of Light, nor on the Central Heat of the Earth.

Every Subject under the Sun, although invisibly small contains Life or fire, and of course the four Elements. Now if every Subject contains Heaven or fire, so every Subject has a Motion, whether visible and perceptible or not, yet there is a Motion in it.

Heaven never rests: it must have a Motion, let it proceed from what means it will; and although this principle may seem to be inactive or at rest, yet it has its invisible influences, virtues, and powers.

For instance, a plant, root, or herb, ore or mineral tore from the Spot where it grew, seems to be dead, because it is hindered from growing to a further perfection; But as Heaven is within which is never at rest, it still continues to show its powers and virtues, when that plant or ore is rendered medicinal.

The Lover of Natural Truths sees here, from whence each Concrete derives its power, viz. from the implanted Heaven within as from without, from its perpetual Motion, warmth and heat. Therefore you will look in vain for a Subject big, or even so small which is deprived of Life, that is of Heaven air, water and earth. It stands to reason that the Children resemble Father and Mother, now as all Things did proceed from the Primeval Chaos, they must partake of the same properties. This property was fire and Humidity, but fire is the mover.

Thus fire or the spirit is diffused through the whole system of Nature, so that the meanest drop of water, or the smallest atom of Sand or Earth is filled with that Universal spirit.

Observe here that the whole difference of Things consists only in volatility or fixity; that is: volatility and fixity causes the changes and different modulations of Matter, and the whole scope of Nature is to corporify and fix Heaven, in order to become useful and salutary; which, Heaven could not effect if it were not by the gradual Mediums of Vapours, as it must communicate with the Earth by means of air and water. God has ordained it wisely, that Heaven must become corporeal and be converted into all the Elements, as vice versa, the inferior Elements are by subtilisation converted into air and fire or Heaven, in order to be reimpregnated and renewed by the Celestial Influences, for the sake of generation, preservation, destruction, and regeneration of all Things. We have explained to you how Vapours are converted into air and air into fire, we will now examine the nature of these Vapours.

We have told you that there exists in the Earth an Innate Heat, which we believe to be the strongest in the Center of the Earth, by reason of its swift motion. This Celestial Heat causes a continual transpiration and sublimation of Vapours; such Vapours are Dews and Fogs; these Vapours are two-fold and four-fold. Two-fold because they consist of water and earth, fourfold as they contain the 4 Elements, which four Elements cannot do without each others assistance; that I call these Vapours water and earth is, because they contain those two Elements volatilised and subtilised, and if they ascend they are still further subtilised and converted into air and fire or Heaven.

Such Vapours have been water will be easily admitted, but that they also contain a subtilised earth, may perhaps be doubted; but note, that I have said before, that one Element is the conductor of the other, and that one Element dissolves and subtilises the other.

Fire dissolves and subtilises air, air dissolves and subtilises water, water dissolves and subtilises and mollifies the earth, vice versa, the earth condenses the water, water condenses air, air condenses or corporifies Heaven or fire, by which means air becomes animated, as we have explained before, and becomes this Spiritus Mundi.

Thus one Element is the others Magnet, solvent, volatilising, condensing, coagulating and fixing principles. You are to note here that Nature has its degrees of Volatility and Fixity; as for instance, that part of fire which is nearest to the atmosphere is not so highly pure or subtil, as that which is a thousand leagues remote from it: In the same manner, the highest atmospheric air is purer, colder and more subtil as well as dryer than that air near us, which we breathe. The superfluities of the water is also lighter, more aerial and more subtil than the thick slimy ground waters, which settle on pebbles. stones corals, and covering them with a slime or subtil mud.

The Earth has also its degrees of subtility and fixity: We have therein earth juices, sulphurs, bituminous substances, such as the pitcoal, clays, loams, minerals, ores and metals, rocks, stones, and flints, and the precious gems of a wonderful fixity. The most volatile earth is mollified and dissolved by water, further volatilised into air and fire.

Vice Versa the lowest fire sooner mixes and corporifies itself with the air, than the remote, whilst the lowest atmospheric air sooner mixes with, and becomes water, than the pure and highest air, the Inferior slimy ground waters become earth sooner than the superficial lighter waters.

The Volatile soluble Earth, in particular its Virgin earth, i.e., its salt is sooner dissolved by water than a pebble or Sand. The volatile water is sooner converted into the lower air than the grownd waters can possibly be.

If you understand us right, we shew you here the first beginning of Nature, and the true First Matter. As the 4 Elements proceed from the primordial Vapours, they are forced to generate continually such a Vapour, of the very selfsame principles and substances, which Vapour is converted by Nature into a Chaotic water, and falls down in Showers of Rain.

In this Chaotic water is invisibly contained the Universal Sperm for the generation, preservation, destruction and regeneration of all Things.

Now we have treated of the regeneration of the Chaos or Universal Vapours: we shall further show you its power and virtue so that you may touch it with your hands, as well as see it with your eyes.

Chapter 10

Discovery of the Genuine Universal Sperm In the Regenerated Chaos, the Corporified Animal or Spiritus Mundi

We have demonstrated how fire water air earth be proceed from the first Chaotic Waters, and how they produce the Universal Sperm, and how they continually regenerate the Chaotic waters for generation, preservation and Regeneration of all Things. This Universal Sperm is generated by condensation and evaporation of Vapours, which are circulated in the great Alembic of the Air, until they are sufficiently impregnated or animated by fire, when they are again condensed and resolved into water.

This Chaotic Waters are commonly called Dew, Rain, Showers, Hail, Snow: But really and truly it is the true regenerated Chaos, the genuine spirit and Anima Mundi animates it, who generates, preserves, kills, and regenerates all sublunary Creatures agreeably to their original form, by means of their Seed or Sperm, and this Anima Mundi is Nature truly.

Now to prove that this Dew. Rain, Hail. or Snow is actually the regenerated Chaos, containing the Universal Sperm and spirit Mundi we must show you that they were generated first out of the primordial Chaos. We must also show, nay, we have done it before, that our regenerated Chaos contains the four Elements, and if it contains them, it must of course possess all what the four Elements contain.

We say therefore as a fundamental truth, that everything can be resolved and must return to that; what it was at first; and everything must be resolved and be returned to its first origin by that self-same principle by which it was made or generated naturally. The Elements originate from Vapour and fire, and they return to Vapour, that is

Water, and from thence to fire. They proceed from fire and humidity, and by fire and humidity they return to their first origin.

Now that Dew and Rain is fire and water, or such a regenerated Chaos as the first Chaos was, is proved by its visible effects, better known to Country-men and Gardeners than to Citizens: Chemical Anatomy demonstrates visibly that the four Elements are contained in Dew and Rain water.

Daily experience confirms it, that by the effects of those waters every Plant prospers and grows, Animals cannot do without it, and minerals and metals are generated by their inward fiery principle, as we shall show hereafter. Now let us examine this Universal Sperm, or regenerated Chaotic water by Chemical Anatomy. Take a quantity of Dew, Rain, Snow or Hail, which you like; but the most expeditious way is if you take Rain water from a thundershower, receive it into clean glazed earthen Vessels, and filter it in order to separate the dirt from it which intermixes from the Roofs of Houses, and you will after filtration, have a clear crystalline water, of no particular taste, in fact a fine clear water, fit to be used like any other water.

Place this collected water in a warm garret, where neither Sun nor Moon can shine upon it, cover the Vessels with a Linen Cloth, to prevent the dust getting into it.

Let it stand a month unmoved, and if the place is warm enough, you will by this time perceive an alteration in the water, because this water begins by the power of the implanted fire or spirit grow warm although imperceptibly and to break; it begins to ferment and putrefy and acquires a bad smell, and you will observe that it becomes turbid, although it was perfectly clear at first, and a brown spongy earth ascends swimming at the top, which increases daily and from its weight falls to the bottom.

Here you see a separation, occasioned by the ingrafted spirit of the gross from the subtil.

The separated earth is brown, spongy or like wool slimy and slippery, and this slimy earth is the Universal Gur of Nature.

Here the Artists may observe two things viz. water and earth, which conceal fire and air.

Here the air animated by the fire is extended in the water. Now you have two passive Elements water and earth. In the beginning you had only a volatile water but by a gentle putrefaction in a warm place you have manifested the earth also. Fire and air we must look for in another way.

When you see now your Rain water in that state of putrefaction that the slimy Earth is separated and falls to the bottom. then stir it up with a clean wooden handle.

Separation and Distillation

Now pour your troubled water and earth in that state of putrefaction into a large Glass Body, which place in an earthenware pot, fixed into a charcoal distilling furnace, apply a large alembic and receiver and light your fire, which keep so gentle that only the stream or vapours arise. Let this all come over first as a pure water, which contains animated air, that is air and fire. Distil no more of the very volatile water over; than what will go with the gentlest degree of Heat, whilst the Subject in the body only vapours away but must not be suffered to boil, in this manner you vapour over about the fourth part of the whole, or less.

Take the receiver off with this very volatile water, this water the more so, if you afterwards rectify it per se over a steam bath is more luminous and clearer than common distilled water, which is a proof that it contains much air and fire.

Now apply another receiver and continue the distillation, raising your heat sufficiently, so as to cause the thickish water in the Glass Body to boil and in this manner you must distil all the water over, which will appear like water and in drops in the Alembic; continue the distillation until it remains in the body like melted Honey and looks Brown, but beware of distilling until it remains dry, because you would burn the young and tender Virgin earth in the bottom of the Vessel, which is not yet fixt. Take the distilled water away and put it by as the Element water.

The Honey-like Matter, or the moist earth remaining in the Glass body, take out cleanly and put it into a china basin and set it in the Sun to evaporate until it is perfectly dry; then grind it in a Glass Mortar to a subtil earth. Now you have separated the Elements out of your Chaos.

Now it remains to be proved that they are truly Elements or else it must be false what I have written, that all sublunary subjects proceed from them. To produce heavenly subjects out of this Chaos, or meteors, as this water itself is a meteorical production, let no one undertake; but we will demonstrate that Animals. Vegetables and Minerals may, and can be generated, and that is what we pretend and no further.

To Generate Minerals

Take your dried earth put it into a glass Body and humect it a little with a few drops of your Dist: water, but not with the Element air and fire, and put the Body in a warm room facing the South, but let not the Sun's Rays shine upon the Body; after your earth is dry, humect or imbibe it again with the Element water. then set it to dry, and this humecting and drying you may repeat several times every day and continue so doing during the whole Summer, and you can mineralise the whole Earth. You will find by your inbibitions and exsiccations, that the Earth becomes more ponderous and sandy.

NB. the Glass Body must be covered with paper only to keep the dust out, as there must be left access of air. As soon as you perceive that the earth is become sandy, you may know that it is mineralised, this sandy earth is neither Animal nor Vegetable, consequently Mineral. If you have a few ounces of this earth, try it as Glauber tries the sun containing Sands and you will find a grain or two of sun and moon.

To Produce Vegetables Out of Your Earth

Take your before mentioned earth dried in the Sun. put it into a Glass Body, make a mixture of two parts of water and one part of air (which you rectified in the beginning) with this humect or unbibe your earth as the gardeners do, by sprinkling only, not too wet, not too dry, place your Body (open) on the air not so that the Sun can shine upon it, and you will find several Vegetables productions spring up in a few weeks, although you have sown no Seed.

If you like to produce Animals. Take your before mentioned dried and powdered earth, pour first together, one part of water, and three parts of air, with this mixture humect your earth so copiously that it may become like liquid or melted Honey, place the Glass body which contains this mixture in the Air where it is warm, the Sun may shine on it but not too hot, nor at the Meridian, and the Glass is left open.

You will perceive that in a few days, there will be different kinds of small vermine, in the thick water ; when the earth diminishes and dries up you must humect it again, so that it may remain of the same consistence like Honey or Syrup, as before; and you will perceive that the first small vermine will die and loose themselves, and others will be produced who will feed on their putrefaction and become larger and more in number.

I could reveal here something, but as it would be abused by profligate men, I am obliged to be silent.

You may be convinced by these experiments that our water or regenerated Chaos, Rain water, or Dew, or Snow is, and contains the Mundi and Universal Sperm, out of which, all things were, and are generated. It appears from this that this water and Earth are endowed with the principle of fertility for the three departments of Nature, as all things are produced thereof.

Few there are that know the secret powers of these things, and what it is that causes and gives fertility!

It is a spirit or fire, but as a volatile unembodied spirit, he can effect nothing in natural productions.

All what is to be serviceable in visible Bodies, must be, or become corporeal with them, it must become visible and palpable: therefore this great and wonderful Universal spirit must take a visible and palpable Body, as well as the Animal and Vegetable Sperm is visible and palpable. Few know this although they handle it often enough.

This corporified Anima Mundi or Universal Sperm according to its origin is but little known, although it may be got in great quantity. The cause of this obscurity is that it bears a different name from what it ought to have. According to its root and origin it ought to be called the Sperm of the Macrocosm, the Sperm of the World, the cause of Fertility. This title belongs to it as it is the concentrated corporified Sperm, and spirit Mundi in a transparent visible crystalline Body, a dry water, which does not wet the hands, an earth, a fiery pure earth, full of Light and fire also full of cold, like ice, a coagulated or congealed fire, a condensed and animated air, which is better and more valuable than all the Treasures in the World!

But that I may show You this embodied spirit and that you may touch It with your hands, proceed as I teach you. Process to demonstrate the corporified Anima Mundi!

Take your putrefied Rain water, put it into a large glass Body cut off low, or into a china basin of a large size, which place in an earthenware pot, and evaporate this putrefied water gently, until there remains only a 1/3 part of the whole. Let the fire die away whilst it is yet luke warm, filter it through blotting paper. Pour the clear into a clean pewter basin, or into an earthen glazed dish, which place in a cool Cellar or Room, and during the night the celebrated Spiritus Mundi will shoot in Crystals and appear under two different forms.

The first is of a perfect crystalline transparent form, this shoots ah round the sides of the Basin and settles on small sticks. if you place any on the water.

The second fixes itself on the bottom of the Basin, and is darker and not so transparent.

Here now you see that celebrated spirit, the Universal spirit, the Sperm of the Macrocosm, the regenerated Chaos visible and bodily. Pour the water off gently, and let the crystals dry. Those crystals which hang all round the sides or on the sticks keep by themselves separately. Those that are fixed on the bottom of the Basin keep separately also.

With both sorts of crystals go to old Lame Vulcan and he will tell you their Names! Take some of those Crystals which hung all round the sides of the Basin, or were fastened to the sticks and throw them on lighted Charcoal, and they will tell you what they are, They are called nitre.

The bottom Crystals throw also on fiery Coals, they have a harsh voice and spit about them. They are called Common salt or Alkaline salt.

Here you have both names of the Corporified spirit Mundi!

This nitre out of the Rain water fulmunates with sulphur, like any other Salpetre, and has no other, or greater effect than Common purified universal seed.

The salt cracks and flies from the fiery coals like any other Common salt, and shows the same effect in all other operations like good Common salt. By this experiment you may perceive clearly the Center and Sperm of all things, the Sperm of the World, visibly and corporified before your eyes, and you may touch it with your hands! Both generate, preserves, destroy and regenerate everything that is on Earth.

In the atmosphere it is volatile and incorporeal, and produces volatile meteors in water and earth, it assumes a crystalline Body. and produces corporeal Subjects. according to different degrees of fixity; no objects under the sun in their last resolution are found without one or the other.

Everything in Nature does consist of these two.

The one is Nitre	The other is Salt
The one is Acid	The other is Alkaline
The one is Spirit	The other is Body
This is the Father	This is the Mother
This is the Male Sperm	This is the Female Sperm
This is the Universal Agent	This the Universal Patient
Primordial Sulphur	Primordial Mercury and Salt
Fire and Air	The Magnet
Chalybs Sendivogii	The Magnet
The Hammer	The Anvil
Sulphur Naturae	Mercury and Salt Naturae

In the beginning this Chaotic water was entirely Volatile, because if you did distil it before putrefaction, every drop of it ascends like volatile water; By fermentation and putrefaction it gets a basis of fixation and precipitates its subtil earth.

The most volatile part of this water generates Animals, when it becomes a little fixer it generates Vegetables, and when it becomes quite fixed it generates Minerals and Metals. Whosoever like to generate minerals, let him take the fixest parts, such as eath and water. If you like to produce Vegetables, add to the earth and water some air and fire. If you want to bring forth Animals add still more of the most volatile, that is more air and fire, as containing more of the Universal. The vegetable department stands between Animals and Minerals. because out of them a Mineral or Stone may as soon be produced as an animal, as we shall show hereafter.

The efficient cause which has enabled us to see and feel the Universal Corporified Sperm, is putrefaction, the Principal Key whereby the Lock of Natural Subjects may be opened.

The cause of fermentation and putrefaction is the implanted spirit which is never idle whenever he meets with Humidity, his own instrument, by means of which this spirit is ever busy, either visibly or invisibly, either sensibly or insensibly, this causes fermentation and putrefaction; and out of a volatile makes a fixt, and out of a fixt again a volatile and this mutation is continued without ceasing.

This spirit breaks and dissolves Stone and Rocks, which he himself has coagulated and reduces them into Sand and Dust; this same spirit reduces Trees into Mould and earth, and putrefies Animals, and again from such putrefied substances produces Vegetables and Minerals, and this continues from one thing into another.

I have said that the Universal Corporified Sperm of the World, produced out of the regenerated Chaos of Rain water, that is our nitre and salt is not better than common nitre, and common salt, and it is truly so because they produce the same effect and operation, and their is no difference between them, except if the one should be more purified than the other, but if they were equally pure, there could be no difference; therefore let the Artist not be deceived, if anyone would tell him, this from the Chaotic water is the nitre of the Philosophers, and the other is vulgar nitre, we say that such a distinction is folly and superstition.

If Common pure nitre produces the same effects as the other does, then Common nitre is philosophical nitre; but that the Reader may be convinced that the Universal nitre out of the Rain water is not better than purified vulgar nitre, let him consider that the Universal nitre is the Father and Generator of vulgar nitre, and he must then naturally conclude that the Blood of the Infant must be like that of Father and Mother, and that it must contain the very same principles and consequently must produce the same effects as the Father, nay, it is itself the Father, and is centrally one and the same with the Father and omnipresent.

Now if out of the Universal nitre and salt all things are produced. Animals, Vegetables and Minerals, all things of course are reducible into these their first principles. and still further into Vapour. That all things proceed from universal seed is demonstrated by nitre and salt being found everywhere in all things.

Chapter 11

That Nitre and Salt are Found In the Air and In All Things In This World

As we cannot ascend towards the heavenly Bodies, we must judge of what is above by that which is below within our reach. The Firmament is full of Light, Light is nothing else but attracted and repulsed, moved and manifested fire of Nature or Universal spirit. This further agitated and concentrated produces Heat and fire. Nitre is coagulated fire concealed in air and Humidity; therefore we say and conclude, that the Heavens or intermediate Space between us and the Heavenly Bodies consists of, or is filled with a most volatile incorporeal nitre, which as it descends into our Atmosphere and probably other atmospheres of Heavenly Bodies becomes gradually more and more corporeal. Let this suffice concerning the Spiritual Heavenly nitre. That there is nitre and salt in the Air is plain by lightning, thunder and Hail. Here on Earth we cannot find another subject which fulminates, thunders, and hails besides nitre or stalteous things.

Nitre is born spiritual and volatile in the Heavens, in the atmosphere it becomes acid but remains spiritual and volatile, in water and earth it assumes a visible and palpable Body; how that happens that it inflames hails, fulminates and thunders in the atmosphere, we will first demonstrate theoretically by physical reasons, and then mechanically by practice.

Nitre does not fulminate, except it meets with a contrary agent and is excited by heat.

The more volatile and subtil the nitre is, the more vehemently it fulminates and is the easier enflamed.

In the same manner volatile and subtil its contrary agent is the more vehement, sudden and powerful in their mutual operation.

The Light heavenly fire and Life of all things is condense in the atmosphere in the form of a subtil volatile nitre and this must have a contrary agent for its operation.

In order that this volatile nitre may obtain a contrary agent, there ascends continually out of the Earth, Ocean and Rivers an equally subtil, volatile, sulphureous, alcaline Earth in the shape of Vapours, Fumes, and Fogs, filled with salt alcalicum Volatile. This is the natural evaporation of the Earth excited by the Central heat of the Earth. This ascends continually to meet the Volatile incorporeal nitre, now, when they do meet in a dry rarified atmosphere they are moved by the Sun's Rays, which by those ascending Vapours are collected and concentrated, whereby these Vapours become more and more heated until the subtil nitre takes fire and fulminates with this contrary sulphureous, volatile, alcaline agent, rarefies the air all round and thunders with dreadful Explosions as we observe during hot, dry, Summer days.

When on the contrary the atmosphere is dense and loaded with humidity, these two Universal Agents meet peaceably: the subtil nitre joins itself and embraces quietly the volatile sulphureous alcali without any vehement concussions: as is the case in Winter, when Humidity and Cold prevail in our atmosphere. Humidity and Cold hinder the inflammation and, consequently the fulmen.

Take nitre let it melt in a crucible, in an open fire, add to it a volatile alcaline sulphureous nitre, such as sal ammoniac or volatile nitre of urine, which is also sulphureous, or a volatile earth. Such are Charcoal, Mineral sulphur, Vegetable and Animal Oils, and the nitre will take fire and fulminate like gunpowder; the more volatile the earth or the nitre is, but in a dry state, the more violently does the nitre fulminate, and this reaction takes place only in a dry heat, but in humidity they unite peaceably and quietly. Humidity is here a third Medium which prevents the fulmen.

If you dissolve volatile salt of urine, or sal ammoniac with nitre in water, both are dissolved without violence or alteration, but if this humidity or water is evaporated and coagulated over the fire to dryness, so that they only commence to melt, they inflame and fulminate immediately. Another evident proof we have in Aurum fulminans.

The reason of its fulmen many have sought to explain, but few have known it.

Many chemists have attributed this fulmen to the sun itself: some to compressed air, but here is the true reason:

The Fulmen Explained

Sun is dissolved in aqua regia, which must contain com. nitre or sal ammoniac in order to become aqua regia. The sun when dissolved is precipitateted with fixt oil of tartar or with any other alcali, such as a volatile salt of urine, or so-called spirit of urine, and the Sol falls to the bottom as a Spongy quicklime.

Although this quicklime is edulcorated or washed a 100 times with water, yet you will not take its fulmen from it by washing because some of the vinegar and alcaline salt remain fixed therein so that such a sun quicklime becomes heavier than the sun employed. Now let us examine the quicklime or sun fulminans.

It is on the same foundation of nitre and sal ammoniac dissolved in, and then evaporated to dryness, with this difference, that here in the progress of the sun fulminans, the ingredients or principles are subtilised, and in the former solution only crude. The aqua regia is composed of aqua fortis and sal ammoniac or Sea salt; aqua fortis is spirit of nitre, the oil of Tartar for the precipitation is a fixt alchali. Now when the sun is dissolved in the aqua regia containing a highly volatile nitre by means of sal ammoniac as being a volatile alcaline earth it is then precipitated with the oil of Tartar, which is a subtil fixt alcaline earth, the vinegar spirit in the aqua fortis are here partly saturated, precipitated and fixed by the salt of Tartar their enemy and contrary, and as this fixt salt is more porous than the earth of sun, it lets go the sun after having impregnated it first strongly with fixt vinegar nitreous and volatile alcaline spirits, as much as the atoms of sun will receive; for that reason it precipitates the sun to the bottom and detains it as an earth. Every dry earth is greedy to receive a salt, arid as these two salts of the aqua fortis and sal ammoniac are very subtil and volatile they are easily excited and inflamed by the least motion or smallest Heat: as soon as they feel that, Heat, they fulminate and break forth downwards, as gunpowder shows its greatest force upwards. Thus the volatile nitre and volatile alcali in the sal ammoniac as powerful Re-agents cause the fulmen and explosion and not the sun.

The cause of the sun's explosion downwards is because it is a fixed earth which inclines downwards, whilst the charcoal in the gunpowder being a volatile sulphureous earth explodes upwards.

We also observe a great difference between the force of the explosion of sun fulm, and of common gunpowder, the explosion of sun fulm being three times as violent as that of gunpowder because in the sun fulm is a spiritual volatile highly subtilised nitre, whilst the gunpowder is composed of crude corporeal nitre; therefore the more subtil, volatile and spiritual the counter-agents are, the greater must be the effect.

If you precipitate to the sun quicklime, in the room of taking a fixt alcali such as the oil Tartari pr. delig. with a subtilised, volatilised alcali, such as a salt volatile urineae or a vol: salt of Hartshorn, the fulmen and explosion will be still more violent. Thus we have demonstrated that the fulmen and explosion proceeds from the Universal principles and not from the sun.

On the contrary if you want to take the fulminating power from the sun quicklime, proceed in this way; After having well washed your sun fulm., let the humidity drain from it on blotting paper; then make a strong alcaline lye of fixed salt of Tartar and water, or of pure potash and water, or oil of Tartar and water, and boil your sun fulminans is such a lye for about 15 or 20 minutes, then wash and dry the quicklime and its fulmen is entirely gone and lost.

The reason of this phenomenon is, that the fixt alcaline lye dissolves the volatile vinegar and alcaline counter-agents, which had fixed themselves in the golden earth, and dissolving them destroys their union, and by its fixity destroys the power of fulminating anymore.

From all this it appears plain that the fulminating quality proceeds from volatile nitre and a subtil, volatile alcali or a volatile sulphureous earth, such as the charcoal sulphur, and the more volatile those agents are, the stronger is the fulmen; and the fixer they are, the less the fulminate. If you project an oil, sulphur, charcoal dust, arsenic, [unidentified symbol], antimony, etc. into fluid nitre, they repel each other and cause a violent reaction according to the volatility and oiliness of the projected agent.

On the contrary, if you project common nitre or fixed salt of Tartar or any fixed alcali, or a fixed earth, such as terra sigillata, chalk, quicklime, which contains nothing volatile into melted nitre, you will see no re-action, but they will soon unite peaceably and fix each other, without fulminating. We have now proved theoretically and practically that there is a volatile nitre and salt in the air, and that the fulmen proves it, as well as the experiment with thunder-rain water.

Chapter 12

That There Is Nitre and Salt In All Waters and Earths

That nitre and salt is in Rain water we have proved by an Experiment. That it is in all earths and waterss can easily be demonstrated.

If you take any earth whether from fields, meadows, marshes, Hills or Valleys, a sufficient quantity, and dissolve as much as you can of such an earth in distilled Rain water, and then filter the solution and evaporate it, until there remains no more than a third part of the whole quantity of water employed, the pour it off into basins or dishes and let it stand to cool over night in a cold place, and you will find crystals of nitre and salt in a lesser or greater quantity, according as the Earth was less or more impregnated with nitre and salt. The Saltpetre boilers understand this best as they boil no earth but such as is rich in nitre, to pay them for their labour.

It is the same with all Waters, springs and wells, which are all more or less impregnated with nitre and salt; nay, some Springs are thoroughly saline and nitreous.

Rivers flow out of the Earth, dissolve the nitre and salt and carry it along with them into the Ocean. Why the Ocean more salt com, than nitre is because the Sun reverberates it continually, principally between the Tropics, where the Rays of Light fall more perpendicularly; this along with the motion occasioned by the Winds and Tides convert the Aereal incorporeal nitre into Sea salt; it looses its fulmen and becomes alcaline.

Experiment

Take nitre with its own earth, before it is purified, and boil it often in water, until it is dry, and increase your heat more and more as you advance with your boilings, and you will see that the Nitre loses gradually its Fulmen and becomes more and more fixed, until after 40 or 50 boilings it becomes quite fixed and alkailsed and fulminates no more, but is converted into common salt. Therefore we say that Common or Sea salt is nothing else but nitre originally, reverberated and alcalised by the Rays of Light.

Fixation In Via Sicca

This fixation of nitre is done more expeditiously with quicklime viva, than by the detonation with charcoal or sulphur.

Take fiery stone lime fresh from the kiln, which reduce to powder and Nitre finely powdered [in equal parts] mix the two powders by rubbing them together in a mortar; 1/2 lb. of each. Put this mixture in a roomy crucible, in a wind furnace and begin your fire gradually (a lid must he luted on which must have a small hole in the middle) let the fire be gentle the first two hours to season the crucible, then keep it moderate during two hours more. so that the Coals lay no higher than the upper part of the ^-. after that i.e. after the first four hours, cover the crucible with Coals and keep up a good fire during four hours more, so that the crucible, keeps always glowing hot like the fiery Coals. Then let the fire go out gradually towards night take out and break the crucible and you will find your nitre alcalised or fixed in a lump which is outwardly Green and inwardly Purple.

Elixivate this mass with hot water, or powder it and let it flow per delig. (this is best).

During the first three or four hours of the operation the vinegar spirit is forcibly driven out of the small hole in the cover and even through the Luting, and displays various beautiful colours on the fiery Cof the Generation o You may also fix nitre if you melt it with common salt [in equal parts] or with fixt nitre of Tartar [in equal parts] and the nitre becomes fixt.

If you let the mass flow per dilig. evaporate your oil of fixt nitre to a dry fat salt,. and melt that, and if you project sulphur or Powdered Charcoal, it does no longer fulminate.

NB. Such a nitre fixes sulphur by degrees.

Chapter 13

That Nitre and Salt Is Found In Animals, That Animals Proceed From Nitre and Salt, and Are Resolved Into Nitre and Salt

Whatsoever is intended to cause fertility must be saline or nitreous. or it can be no manour. All Animals are nitreous or Saline, as by their Chemical Anatomy, by distillation, we find they contain a certain quantity of volatile, and some a fixt salt and a stinking oil or sulphur. The fixt salt appears, when we calcine the ashes. That this animal oil is a liquid salt is proved by its inflammation, because it burns, and nothing can burn but what is either nitreeous, or sulphureous. The fixt salt and fixt earth cannot burn. We have a still stronger proof in the phosphorous made out of animal salts.

That the Animal department is very nitreous is proved by the Saltpetre - boilers in Germany, who dig up the floors of Stables and Cow-houses in the country, such as have been abandoned, and by boiling such an earth, they find it very rich of nitre.

The same is done on old forsaken burying grounds, and they find such an earth, if it has but laid long enough, very rich of nitre, which are sufficient proofs that the animal department is nitreeous, and that animal substances are reduced into nitre; and where into a Concrete is reduced, from that very principle it has its origin, and this Resolution and Mutation is performed bid the Archaeous of Nature, or Universal spirit in the air.

Chapter 14

That Nitre and Salt Is Found In Vegetables; That Vegetables Consist of Nitre and Salt, and Are Resolved Into Nitre and Salt

That Vegetables grow by Dew and Rain out of water and earth is known to all husband-men and gardeners.

We have shown you that the pure and real essence of Dew and Rain nitre and salt, and that all waters and earths do conceal either one or both. Now it is known that the Universal Sperm, that is. Dew, Rain, Snow or rather the nitre and salt concealed therein causes fertility and the growth of Vegetables; nitre and salt are found in all waters and earths if this be true, it is also true that Vegetables grow and live by those salts, as a pure or empty earth or an empty water without Sperm are insufficient for their production and preservation, and this sperm is nothing else but nitre and salt.

Experiment

Take two parts of salt and one part of nitre, melt these two together in a roomy crucible. When cold, beat the mass into a powder, and dissolved 1 lb. weight of it in 10 lbs. of Rain water, keep this for use. In this water soak any seeds, until then swell, then dry them in the Sun, and sow them in the ground. Now take some of the same Seeds not soaked in this Spermatic water, and sow them close to the others, but mark both places. You will soon perceive the sudden growth of the soaked Seeds the beauty of the Fruit and the quantity in comparison to the unprepared seeds. If you will pour about a quart of the above water to the root of a Fruit tree or Vine, and repeat that once a month, for instance in Febr: March and April, you will perceive a wonderful fertility of that Tree that Season.

That Vegetables are very nitreous in general yet some more than others, appears by their Ardent spirit, or so-called S.V., by their Vinegar, by their oiliness and alcaline salt. We see Vegetables break forth into a strong Flame when they are set on Fire.

Inflammability, Heat and Flame proceed from nitre and sulphur and from nothing else.

Is not the spirit Ardens or S.V. a subtil and heavenly nitre? It burns so beautifully like the splendour of the Stars. That the oil contains a salt is demonstrated by their alcali, whereby they dissolve sulphurs.

We have also given satisfaction to this department and have proved that their First Matter is nitre and salt, that is, their Universal not yet specificated Matter, which when united universal seed generate all things.

Chapter 15

That Nitre and Salt Is Found In Minerals; That Minerals Are Formed of Nitre and Salt, and Are Resolved Into Nitre and Salt

The more the Universal fire of Nature approaches the earth, the more it becomes terrestrial and corporeal; the more it becomes corporeal, it becomes more fixt, and the more fixt it is, the less it is inflammable; thus nitre descends from Heaven is volatile and incorporeal, although visible in Light, and concealed in the water, out of which it becomes manifest by putrefaction.

The more terrestrial and fixer this nitre becomes the more it is alcalised, and looses gradually its fulminating power, as appears in minerals and metals; because the more it descends from its Universal Nature, the more it alters its Nature and quality, and assumes a different nature in Animals, a different character in Vegetables, and different quality in minerals and Metals; yet it manifests its fiery nature in all three, more or less, according to its degree of volatility of Fixity; in the Animal and Vegetable departments in Oils, Fats, Resin, Pitch, and in the Minerals in sulphureous substances, such as sulphur etc.

As the Minerals are of a Stony nature and descend gradually to more and more fixity, the inflammable sulphur by gradual and continued fixation is deprived of its inflammability and obtains another quality, and incombustible one.

That sulphur and such like adustable substances are of a nitreous origin we have demonstrated before and proved, that all inflammability proceeds from nitre. That there is a salt in Minerals is perceived, when we elixivate a mineral with water, after having glowed it previously in the fire; but that such a mineral salt is not always found in any considerable quantity and sometimes hardly perceptible, is the reason, because it becomes more and more terrestrial, and the more earth it dissolves; the more it forsakes its original Saline nature, at to outward appearance.

We see plainly, that, if we wish to separate the firmly united mineral and metallic Bodies, we are obliged to make use of Saline and nitreous Menstrums, without which they cannot be opened, and that every menstrum is either saline, nitreous, or mercurial, every good chemist knows. Therefore as the minerals meet and dissolve in a saline menstruum it is evident that they must possess a nature which is congenial to Salt or nitre, or they could not be conquered thereby; thus they can be resolved into a Saline or nitreous Nature, therefore such is also their first origin.

After having dissolved a Metallic Body in a Saline Menstruum, if you evaporate your Solution to a third part, the solution will shoot into a salt or vitriol, which vitriol by distillation and cohobation becomes an vinegar, ponderous spirit or oil from or out of which they proceed at first; because all minerals and metals proceed originally and are generated from an acid, fermented, putrefied nitre and salt, which dissolve a suitable Earth and from vitriol, sulphur, marcasit, metal; which is done by a gradual fixation and nourishment by the original nitreous and saline spirits thus as they were generated by an acid, fermented spiritual nitre and salt, they are resolved by them and brought back to their First Matter.

Table of Generation
Anima Mundi

Fire

in

Nitre and Salt

United and fermented become

acid and Corrosive

dissolve a suitable Earth

and form

A vitriolic Soft butyraceous Gur; The above Vapours becoming more and more corrosive retain their androgynal nature of Nitre and Salt and constitute now a double sulphureous and arsenical or mercurial Vapour

this setting by corroding forms nature
vitriol, sulphur, arsenic,
and by succeeding sulphur vapours, and also arsenical
Vapours, they form and generate

When Sulphur predominates	When Arsenic predominates
Sulphurous Macarsites	Arsenical, Marcasites, Cobalt
Pyritis, Antimony etc, Wolfram etc.	Bismuth etc.
Mars Venus Sun	Saturn Jupiter Moon

When both principles are in equality
they form [unidentified symbol] cinnabar mercury

Mercury

The Body of saturn, jupiter, moon, and with more sulphur of Mars, Venus, Sun, Platina I think is of a Solar nature from its weight and fixity.

Minerals are generated from nitreous and saline waters, which penetrate into the Earth through its pores and crevices, this nitreous saline water is heated and fermented by the ascending central heat of the Earth, is resolved into Vapours and forced upwards again towards the circumference but by this continual circulation, these Vapours are resolved again into water and ferment more and more, whereby they are subtilised, rendered more acid and corroding.

These fermented waters as they contain a subtil spirit of nitre and salt, they become more and more corrosive; if they were not corrosive, who could they dissolve Stones and Rocks?

Therefore this Corrosive water dissolves Rocks, Stones, and earths which is condensed and coagulated again by the gentle subterraneous Heat into Salt, but not into such a Salt as it was in the atmosphere or in the Ocean, but into a Vitriolic Salt, which by succeeding vapours is formed into a subtil, corrosive, smeary or unctuous earth, which the Miners all Gur.

This Gur is by succeeding Vapours dissolved and filled with corrosive Acidity until it is changed into native sulphur; because the more corrosive it receives, the more sulphureous it becomes; but when the Mercurial Alcaline Vapours of Sea salt predominate over the nitreous Sulphureous Vapours, the Universal Gur goes over into arsenic, which is a dry mercury. Both sulphur as well as arsenic, by fixation and succeeding Vapours become Marcasite, such as antimony, Cobalt, Bismith, Wolfram, etc. this Marcasite is the first and nearest Matter toward Metals, and not vitriol, which is the remote first Matter of Minerals and Metals. That Sulphur is very corrosive, in plainly perceived by its Smell, which is suffocating, when received in the lungs, and by its spirit and oil which is a strong corrosive. We see that the spirit and oil of vitriol are dissolved sulphureous vinegar, if you imbibe a fixt earth, such as chalk therewith, and suffer the vinegar to evaporate strongly from that earth in an open fire, you will see an inflammation and burning like that of common sulphur. That sulphur has been a nitreous salt, appears from its vinegarspirit which is of a Universal mineral nature. When this vinegarspirit has forsaken the Body of the sulphur, there remains an unctuous earth or the First Universal Mineral Gur behind, in small quantity.

The reader may judge whether I understand the generation of Minerals or not: Let him proceed either towards or backwards in the

Anatomy of Minerals, and if he works rightly, he will see what he perhaps did not believe before!

Our ancestors have written that sulphur, mercury and salt are the First Matter of Metals; true philosophers understand this properly; sulphur and mercury proceed from salt and nitre, and metallic salt is vitriol perfected and fixt; we have explained how the earth in the Mines by receiving nitre, or corrosive vinegar becomes sulphur; but the more such an earth is alcalised by nitre, so that the vinegar corrosive is overcome, arsenic, mercury, or Mercurial subject is generated.

Thus it appears plain that nitre and salt are the Sperm of the Macrocosm, volatile and fixed; the visible elements air, water and earth being the vehicle or dwelling of that Universal Sperm. All minerals are generated by an acid corrosive vapour and subterraneous air animated by nitre and salt, by the ancients named sulphur and mercury, because nitre and salt contain the very seminal principles of sulphur and mercury, which vapour and air are circulated and sublimed upwards by the central fire become water and ferment, and by their corrosiveness dissolve a suitable earth and generate the Mineral Gur; and what is it else that performs this generation but the Universal fire of Nature, corporified in nitre and salt.

Chapter 16

Of the Principal Gate Key to Nature, the Author of Destruction and Regeneration of All Things, Called Putrefaction

Heaven or fire; Anima and spirit Mundi is in its own Nature unchangeable, omnipresent, and immortal, but as it gradually unites with humidity, becomes the Universal vinegar and incorporeal Spiritus Mundi, it lends itself then to all those changes the matter or corporified humidity is subsequently liable to, therefore in the air it begins to ferment, and still more so in water and earth, in order to prepare the way for generation; without this fermentation and putrefaction the Universal spirit does generate nothing.

Therefore without previous maceration, fermentation, putrefaction in gentle warmth and humidity, whether it be quick of slow, perceptible or imperceptible, no real or genuine Anatomy of Natural Bodies, whether in Universal or in specificated subjects can be effected.

Dew, Rain, Snow, Hail, Frost, all without distinction ferment and thereby cause a separation of the subtil from the gross, the sign of which is, that a feeble sour smell is perceived.

1. Animals putrify sooner and easier, and on account of their copious, very volatile nitre they emit a most intolerable smell.

2. Vegetables putrefy easily on account of their humidity, yet not so quickly as animals, nor do they smell so badly.

3. Minerals ferment and putrefy, but do not smell so badly as the former two, except mars, which when in real putrefaction smells worse than a corpse.

From this putrefaction we learn that minerals are changed into vegetables, and vegetables into Minerals, and thus Nature changes continually, converting the uppermost into the lowest, and the lowest into the highest, nay, the three Departments of Nature are changed into universal principles. Vapours ascend continually from the Center of the Earth towards the superficies, some of these are fat and sulphureous, and serve the Mineral and Vegetable Departments, and when they penetrate the superficies of the earth, they ascend in Fogs or Mists, and ascending still higher they are Universalised. Exhalations from decayed Trees, leaves, or Vegetables, ascend as well as those from putrid Animal substances and are circulated in the Atmosphere, there to receive the Spiritus Mundi for Reanimation and Chaotisation, which afterwards in the character of regenerated atmospheric air return to Animals by Inspiration, to Vegetables by a magnetic attraction, and to Minerals by their own penetration and assuming a corrosive Nature, as we have explained before.

Few amongst the adolescent Philosophers as well as common self conceited Chemists will put faith in what we say here, but we ourselves are thoroughly convinced that we write the Truth.

Putrefaction or Fermentation are the wonderful Fabricators, which out of earth, produce water, out of water, air, out of air, fire, and convert fire into air, air into water and water into earth earth into Gur, vitriol, sulphur, arsenic, Marcasite, and Metals Nay, the Metals themselves are dissolved and retrograded into vitriol and salt.

This mutation is continued, until it will please God to calcine the whole Earth and vitrifie it into Glass.

Chapter 17

What Putrefaction Is

After God had created by Divine Emanation the Universal fire of Nature, which on account of its essence, being a simple unity not composed of parts, and consequently omnipresent and immortal and which has since time immemorial been justly called the Soul or spirit of the Universe but One in essence, but Threefold in manifestation, resembling its Divine Origin, its Creator; To this Universal Agent, God has given a Power to act by three differently manifested principles.

1. In its omnipresent invisible, most Universal state it has a Universal power of attracting and repulsion, and thereby is the first cause of every Magnetism in the World and of every Celestial Body's keeping in its proper place, as well as of gravitation and falling Bodies in general.

2. In its second manifestation of Light, it has Power to generate Humidity, the firs step towards materiality, to move and ferment that Humidity and thereby to generate the Universal vinegar and to become cold incorporeal Spiritus Mundi, inwardly fire, therewith to animate extended or dilated Humidity, that is atmospheric air, and further to enliven the whole Creation.

3. In this third manifestation of concentrated Light into Warmth, Heat, and burning fire, it does and performs every necessary action what it could not accomplish in its second and first state, nevertheless remaining Centrally always One and the same and omnipresent.

This Universal fire, endowed with an intelligent instinct, called the Universal Agent of Nature, since its first emanation from God, has never been inactive not one moment and produces one alteration after the other, and although it seems to cease in one creature, or recedes from a deceased subject, that same instant it is occupied in producing something else out of such a death or temporal corruption, for which reason the Ancient Philosophers have said "Corruptis unius est generatis alterius." The corruption of one thing brings forth the generation of the other.

This universal fire is the Author and mover of all changes in Natural Things and the Almighty can do with it what He pleases, either for the preservation or destruction of His Creatures.

This Universal spirit begins by Fermentation or by Putrefaction, by this the spirit causes a separation of the pure from the impure, of the most Volatile from the less and least Volatile, of the Subtil from the Gross, when that is done, that same fire unites the pure Volatile again with the less and least Volatile, and rejects what is not wanted for its present purpose.

The above spirit is the Generator, Preserver, Destroyer, and Regenerator of all Things.

When this fire descends into our corporeal Elements, it is detained by them and obliged to assume Body, wherein it appears in a White, cold, crystalline, transparent form nitre, outwardly cold, but inwardly fire; When it inflames, and if there was a sufficient quantity of it and its Enemy should meet him, he would become so irritated, that he would overset an break not only Rocks, but the whole superficies on the Earth.

If its Sister, cold, fixed, Alcali salt, its Venus, whom it loves dearly, which alone can overcome and tame it, was not coexistent and always neat at hand, it nitre would long ago have destroyed the whole Earth.

Its Sister, or Wife, when they embrace each other in Pluto's Fiery Palace does not permit him to do mischief much longer, but lays hold of him by his very Center so that he must convert his Anger ito Love and Friendship.

As soon as he has embraced his Venus and is tied by ties of Love, he forgets his passion totally, so that his Enemies approach him and even lay hold of him he does not show the least inclination to hurt them, on the contrary enters into permanent and everlasting Friendship with them.

This fire or spirit which is all in all Things is distributed in all Creatures, and non can do without it.

Therefore Putrefaction is the First Key and Gate, by means of which the Universal spirit opens to us the Palace containing Natures Secrets.

This spirit is never idle but is continually in action, by action and motion, a warm propriety is communicated; this warmth whether perceptible or not, opens the Pores of all Things, so that the implanted spirit can penetrate everywhere, whether it be corruption or Generation, for Death or Life; after this spirit has penetrated everywhere, it begins to dissolve, and continues until the whole substance is dissolved; the subtil volatile particles evaporate, according to the degree of warmth, and emit a smell, by which we know clearly that the spirit is operating and employed to open the Body by this natural Digestion or Fermentation, and this continues until the proposed end is attained.

This spirit was in the beginning concealed in Vapour and water, and to this moment forms all Things by means of Vapour and Water, and without Humidity of water he generates nothing, because water or Humidity he wants absolutely for his operations, mixings and solutions, as all things mix easily with Humidity or water.

This spirit generates Animals out of Humidity, as Animals consist of humid and soft particles and after the extinction of the fire of Life, they are resolved again into Shine and Humidity, by means of Humidity. It is with Vegetables exactly the same, their juices may be compared to the Fluids in Animals, and their woods and roots to Bones and Cartilages.

Much in the same manner does the Universal spirit generate Minerals by a corrosive water, and removes them again into water by a corrosive water.

The Anima Mundi in its Most Universal State is invisible, and when unmoved, for instance in the flint and steel, and in all things where tranquil, is a cold fire. In its moved volatile state becomes visible in Light, but remains cold, except it is concentrated and further agitated. In its visible state of Light it is called Firmament or Heaven, volatile incorporeal nitre, Ether, Anima, Agent, Male, air; when concentrated and agitated it is Heat fire. When inclining towards corporification it is Universal Acid. When corporified, but remains volatile it is called water, vinegar, Sprit, nitre, salt, vitriol, sulphur, etc. But when it inclines towards fixation it is earth, patient, Body, salt, female, Magnet, and when fixed it is called Alcali, Female Magnet, Void.

This is the true meaning of the Universal spirit and its various forms.

In the beginning it was a simple Vapour or water, animated by fire, which like Protheus assumes various forms and shapes.

Thus we have explained what is the cause of Putrefaction, viz. the implanted fire, the moving, altering, warming, heating, inflaming. separating, omnipresent, simple and homogeneous spirit, but in a double twofold appearance, causing a conflict between Acid and Alcali, sulphur, mercury, salt, Anima, Spirit, Corpus.

www.ingramcontent.com/pod-product-compliance
Lightning Source LLC
LaVergne TN
LVHW041458070426
835507LV00009B/676